KEEP THE BLOOD WARM

Keep the Blood Warm: A 30 Day Guide to a Heart on Fire

Copyright © 2020 by Peter Louis

Scripture quotations are from the ESV® Bible (The Holy Bible, English Standard Version®), copyright © 2001 by Crossway, a publishing ministry of Good News Publishers. Used by permission. All rights reserved.

Scripture quotations marked (NLT) are taken from the Holy Bible, New Living Translation, copyright © 1996, 2004, 2015 by Tyndale House Foundation. Used by permission of Tyndale House Publishers, a Division of Tyndale House Ministries, Carol Stream, Illinois 60188. All rights reserved.

Certain scriptures contain italicized words for emphasis.

ISBN-13: 9798636868026

A Publication of Braveheart Ministries
|| braveheartministries.org

*Printed in the United States of America

KEEP THE BLOOD WARM

A 30 DAY GUIDE TO A HEART ON FIRE

PETER LOUIS

CONTENTS

INTRODUCTION

In a world of distractions it is more important than ever that we learn the rhythms of rest and remembrance. Remembrance is taking time to go into our past to enjoy the faithfulness of God. Remembrance will connect us to the name, nature and goodness of God regardless of our circumstances. We are in a battle every single day! And the battle is for our attention! Because whatever we give our attention to, is what we worship! And we will become what we worship!

When we allow the enemy to control what we look at, what we give our attention to, we give him access to our emotions. And when the enemy starts manipulating our emotions we are tempted to believe that God is far, that he doesn't care for us and that we have been separated from his love and presence. Eventually we become numb to God, through unbelief, all because we gave our attention, continually, to things other than Jesus.

Climbing out of that place of numbness can seem daunting. We feel guilty or responsible for allowing our hearts to wander and so we feel the pressure of trying to work our way back into an awareness of God's love and presence. If this is you, I want to encourage you that you have picked up this guide at just the right time. God wants to show you his nearness! He wants to turn your attention back to the good news that brought you into his presence in the first place!

In this short guided journey, you will discover the simplicity of *first love*. First love is God's love towards you and me demonstrated through the cross. As we will discover, this act of remembrance is an ancient rhythm designed to connect our hearts and minds to the love of God continually. This will result in a personal revival, causing everything we say and do to flow from love!

This is a 30-day guided journey into discovering what it means *to be a holy priesthood, to offer spiritual sacrifices acceptable to God through Jesus Christ."* (*1 Peter 2:5*) We will examine how the Old Covenant priests performed their daily ritual of sacrificing a lamb each morning and at twilight. Through this we will discover the powerful practice of remembrance as we embrace our identity as a holy priesthood. The spiritual discipline of daily remembering, meditating, praying and receiving the love of God expressed through Jesus' atoning work on the cross has transformed my life. By filling my mind, heart and spirit each day with the words of God that describe and explain the *Passion of the Christ* I have more deeply experienced, by the Holy Spirit, righteousness, peace and joy. I have learned to drink from a well that never runs dry and to eat from a table that always satisfies. My hope is to lead you to this altar, the altar of Jesus, and guide you to eat and drink from him every day.

> "We have an altar from which those who serve the tent have no right to eat." (Hebrews 13:10)

Through this spiritual discipline of remembrance, a burning flame has been lit on the altar of my heart and it shall never go out! (Lev. 6:13) It is this flame, this passion and this love that I want to share with you.

HOW TO USE THIS JOURNAL

Each day you will be given two verses about the blood of Jesus and his work as the Lamb of God who takes away the sin of the world! One verse in the morning and one in the evening. The purpose of this journal is to help you slow down each day, connect your heart to the reality of the cross and to position you to bring a pleasing offering to God in light of what Jesus has done for us. Our spiritual health and fruitfulness depends on our ability to remember, receive and abide in God's love for us.

1. Start off by reading the verse slowly, out loud, two or three times. I can't emphasize *slowly* enough. This is not something to check off your list, you have to give the Holy Spirit time to breathe upon what you are reading.
2. If the verse is descriptive in any way, use your imagination to engage the Scripture. Take your time. I will sometimes spend 5-10 minutes simply meditating on each word of the verse until the Spirit illuminates something to me. Often my imagination is sparked in this time and the verse becomes more real to me.

3. Next, write out the verse (*in cursive if you know how*). This will deepen your engagement with the Word and help commit it to memory.

4. Lastly, journal a prayer of thanksgiving or praise to God in light of the verse you have just read. After you have written it out, pray it or sing it out loud to the Father. Oftentimes, after praying the prayer in your journal, you will feel the desire to continue to pour out your heart in prayer or in song...go for it!

For example:

"But now in Christ Jesus you who once were far off have been brought near by the blood of Christ." (Ephesians 2:13)

After you read it out loud, slowly, begin to imagine what it would feel like to be really near to God. How would you feel? Would you feel peace? Joy? Love? Take your time and think about how even though you used to be far away from God, because of Jesus' blood, you are now near to him! That's good news!

Next write out the verse in your own handwriting.

```
But now in Christ Jesus you who once were far
off have been brought near by the blood of
                    Christ.
```

Finally, journal a prayer to God...

```
Father, thank you that I have been brought near
to you by the blood of Christ. When I woke up
this morning, I didn't feel near to you but as
I read your words to me I was reminded you have
brought me near. Your nearness is my good. Help
```

me to stay aware of your nearness throughout my
day. Even though I may not always feel like it,
I know that my nearness to you is based on the
blood of Christ. Thank you for forgiving me of
all of my sins. I never want to forget how
wonderful it is to live with a clean conscience
before you! I love you and I am grateful for
the blood of Jesus. Let my life, my words and
my thoughts today reflect just how thankful I
am to be near to you. Amen.

Remember, if it feels repetitive, you are probably doing it right.
You may not sense or feel anything right away. That is perfectly
normal. Just like starting a diet or working out, it will take some
time to see results. The results that you will begin to see though,
in time, is your heart coming alive to the love of God. You might
cry for the first time in a while. You might feel the warmth of his
presence clothe you as you pray. You might hear his voice of love
and affirmation. You will notice insecurity and the fear of man
beginning to lose its grip on your life. A confidence will be
birthed deep inside of you. Many of you will also notice that
sinful habits such as lust, pornography or media addictions will
begin to dissipate. This is the power of the love of God. This is
the power of the Gospel. This is the power of Jesus. And as we
devote time each day, to remembering and receiving the love of
God demonstrated through the cross, we will become more aware
of his abiding presence and the presence of God is what
empowers us to live the abundant Christian life.

THE SHADOW OF THINGS TO COME

"Now this is what you shall offer on the altar: two lambs a year old day by day regularly. One lamb you shall offer in the morning, and the other lamb you shall offer at twilight." (Exodus 29:38-39)

THE LEVITICAL PRIESTS IN THE OLD COVENANT WERE required to offer two lambs each day. One in the morning and one at twilight. The Levites, the specific tribe of Israel that was tasked with handling the temple duties, were required to do this *daily*. As I was reading this text one morning I was arrested by this verse.

It was as if God himself said, "*Stop, pay closer to attention to what you just read.*" I began to imagine in detail what these two verses looked like each and every day.

The sun is just beginning to rise over the camp of Israel and the sound of bleating lambs and goats fill the morning air. A robed levite rises from his tent and makes his way to the tabernacle. As he enters the outer court he sees the prominent brazen altar. A place of slaughter and forgiveness.

In humble obedience to the temple duties, this levite grabs the yearling lamb. The young male lamb bleats nervously as it is picked up and carried to the place of offering. The priest secures the lamb and he feels the soft wool and tender skin tense up under his grip. As he cuts its throat the lamb lets out a loud bleat, followed by silence. He then finishes the offering by pouring the blood around the altar and burning the animal on the brass grate.

This Spirit-filled vision played over and over in my mind as I imagined the priests performing this duty morning after morning and night after night. As I was pondering how much physical work this required for the priest and the reality of witnessing daily death, it was as if I was awoken from a spiritual slumber. The reality is that the priests would have felt the warmth of the blood of the lamb on their hands and been connected to the weight of the sacrifice each and every day. Whether their hearts connected with it or not, the physical act of taking the life of an animal connected them to the sacrifice in a very intimate way.

I then heard the voice of the Father speak to me:

> "If the priests of the Old Covenant were so diligent in stewarding the blood of lambs, how much more should my New Covenant priests steward the blood of My Son?"

In a moment I realized how numb I was to that reality. How lazy I had been with the blood of Jesus! A deep conviction hit me!

How much of the Christian activity in my life was simply going through the motions instead of a joyous response to the Gospel? How could I be so numb to the greatest act of love the world had ever known?

I started asking myself these questions. What would it look like for me to stay connected to the sobering reality of Jesus' brutal death on the cross? How could I keep the blood of Jesus 'warm' upon my heart? How could I prevent myself from being numb and forgetting the depth of love and the intensity of God's passion for me demonstrated through this moment in time? How do I take something that my mind knows intellectually and move it into a heart reality? How could I, a priest unto God in the New Covenant, keep my heart connected to his sacrifice and from that place offer something of value to God? These questions sparked a deep hunger in me to know how to keep my heart innocent and alive to this truth I had been "taught" my whole life.

This hunger became more than just a neat revelation, it felt as if God was inviting me to partake of an ancient lifestyle that would bring a consciousness of God into my life that I had never known previously. An invitation to enter into my ministry as a priest before God. An invitation to diligently and humbly steward the blood of Jesus Christ. An invitation to be loved deeply and to live a life of love.

NEW COVENANT PRIESTS

WHEN WE TALK ABOUT BEING PRIESTS BEFORE GOD, I THINK many of us simply disconnect from that concept. We don't really know what that means. For us Gentiles, the priesthood is an ancient Jewish reality and has no real bearing on our lives today. But if we look closely, this ancient office holds deep significance for us today. Because for every born again believer, we are called into a holy priesthood!

But what does this priesthood mean for us today? What does it look like practically? We know that God was not pleased or satisfied with burnt offerings offered through the Old Covenant:

> "Sacrifices and offerings you have not desired, but a body have you prepared for me; in burnt offerings and sin offerings you have taken no pleasure." (Hebrews 10:5-6)

So if the old priesthood and the duties they were performing was not pleasing to him, how is our priesthood different? Let's look at a few of the Scriptures that speak of New Testament believers becoming priests.

> "You yourselves like living stones are being built up as a spiritual house, to be *a holy priesthood, to offer spiritual sacrifices acceptable to God through Jesus Christ.*" (1 Peter 2:5)

> "But you are a chosen race, *a royal priesthood,* a holy nation, a people for his own possession, that you may proclaim the excellencies of him who called you out of darkness into his marvelous light." (1 Peter 2:9)

> "and made us a kingdom, *priests to his God and Father,* to him be glory and dominion forever and ever. Amen." (Revelation 1:6)

> "and you have made them a kingdom and *priests to our God,* and they shall reign on the earth." (Revelation 5:10)

So I started thinking about what it would look like to function as a priest in the New Covenant using the shadow of the Old Covenant priestly duties as a guide. It is obvious that the New Covenant does not require us to perform animal sacrifice because Jesus Christ, the Lamb of God, was slain once and for all time. Jesus' blood was sufficient in atoning for the sins of mankind and offering forgiveness for all who would receive it.

So our New Covenant priesthood is based upon the single sacrifice of Jesus, as the Lamb of God. His sacrifice on the cross, is the foundation and source of all of our spiritual activity as priests. What does this mean?

In the Old Covenant system, the condition of the sacrificial lamb was crucial. The lamb had to be spotless and without blemish.

Israel would often get into trouble with God for trying to offer sacrifices that were imperfect. The perfection of the sacrifice was important because if the sacrifice was maimed or blemished, it had no value. And to bring something to God that would otherwise be discarded was considered an offense to God!

So our offerings and sacrifices, as New Covenant priests, must be *connected* to and *grounded* on Jesus' perfect sacrifice. To offer a sacrifice of praise or thanksgiving to God with our lips, while our heart and mind is disconnected from the blood of Jesus, is to offer a blemished sacrifice to God. However, when our hearts are alive to his cross, warmed by his blood and filled with his love, our song of praise and thanksgiving becomes a fragrant offering unto him! It is "strange fire" (Leviticus 10:1) to sing to or minister on behalf of God with a cold heart. So as New Covenant priests, learning to keep our hearts in the love of God becomes paramount for us to experience the abundant Christian life we have been promised (John 10:10).

The entire purpose of this 30-day challenge is to guide you and instruct you in keeping your heart in the love of God and the fellowship of the Holy Spirit. It is designed to help you take what you know in your head and move it into your heart. For many of you, you will discover this numbness lifts almost instantly. While others, it may take a few weeks. Regardless of where you are at, here is my promise:

Accepting this challenge and engaging with this journal will change your life. It will thrust you into an awareness and an experience of God's love that will satisfy you and cause you to hunger for more all at the same time. So if you are ready to take this journey I encourage you to get on your knees and pray something like this:

"Father, I lay these next thirty days of my life before you and I ask that you would meet with me. That you would awaken my heart to your love. I don't want an ounce of numbness towards you or your love for me. I want a fire that will never burn out and that will never grow stale! I am setting my heart to seek you these next thirty days and I am trusting that your grace will sustain me and keep me faithful. If I wander and stray from the path, thank you for lovingly turning my heart and attention back to you. You are a good Father and I trust you with my heart."

SPIRITUAL SACRIFICES

IF THE OLD COVENANT PRIESTS WERE TO OFFER A LAMB every morning and evening, then what do we offer, as New Covenant priests? The Scriptures speak of offering spiritual sacrifices acceptable to God through Jesus Christ. (1 Peter 2:5) What are these spiritual sacrifices? In short, the sacrifices of a New Covenant priest is everything we say and do in light of Jesus' love for us demonstrated on the cross!

WHAT WE DO

"I appeal to you therefore, brothers, by the mercies of God, to present your bodies as a *living sacrifice*, holy and acceptable to God, which is your spiritual worship" (Romans 12:1)

"Do not neglect to do good and to share what you have, for such *sacrifices* are pleasing to God." (Hebrews 13:16)

As priests we have the privilege of presenting our own bodies to God as living sacrifices. To me this represents everything we do in our body, whether it be going to work, raising our kids, loving our spouse, these activities done in the body become worship when we are mindful of Jesus' work in saving us and redeeming us back to God! Paul said it this way, "I have been crucified with Christ. It is no longer I who live, but Christ who lives in me. And the life I now live in the flesh I live by faith in the Son of God, who loved me and gave himself for me." (Galatians 2:20)

Doing good and sharing what we have are also actions that we can take that will please God! But these actions must be done in light of Jesus' love for us. If we try to do good and to share our possessions without remembering and abiding in his love towards us, then the purpose of our sacrifice is usually self-serving. We give to receive. We do good to be praised. These are not actually "sacrifices" that are acceptable to God because they are disconnected from his Son.

WHAT WE SAY

"Through him then let us continually offer up a sacrifice of praise to God, that is, the fruit of lips that acknowledge his name." (Hebrews 13:15)

God loves it when his people praise him! The Psalms say that the Lord is actually enthroned upon the praises of his people! Praise is such a powerful weapon because it invites the authority of God's throne (righteousness and justice) to be established wherever we are and whatever circumstance we find ourselves in. But not all praise is created equal. Praise is personal. Praise comes from the heart. And in order for praise to be praise, it has to be connected to Jesus. In other words, when we speak, sing or declare his praise we must do so with our hearts connected to and abiding in the reality of his sacrifice for us. This is part of our

New Covenant priestly duty, to keep our hearts innocent, alive and abiding in the reality of the steadfast love of God.

Paul hammers this truth home to us by saying, "If I speak in the tongues of men and of angels, but have not love, I am a noisy gong or a clanging cymbal. And if I have prophetic powers, and understand all mysteries and all knowledge, and if I have all faith, so as to remove mountains, but have not love, I am nothing. If I give away all I have, and if I deliver up my body to be burned, but have not love, I gain nothing." (1 Corinthians 13:1-3)

To 'have love' is to have a continual awareness of the cross of Jesus, God's love expressed towards us, constantly sourcing everything we say and do. To not 'have love' is to forget the cross and to live life numb to his passion for us. It is to live a life of unbelief and disconnected from the passion of Christ.

SPIRITUAL FOOD AND DRINK

"'I am the living bread that came down from heaven. If anyone eats of this bread, he will live forever. *And the bread that I will give for the life of the world is my flesh.'*

The Jews then disputed among themselves, saying, 'How can this man give us his flesh to eat?' So Jesus said to them, 'Truly, truly, I say to you, unless you *eat the flesh* of the Son of Man and *drink his blood,* you have no life in you. Whoever *feeds on my flesh and drinks my blood* has eternal life, and I will raise him up on the last day. *For my flesh is true food, and my blood is true drink.* Whoever feeds on my flesh and drinks my blood abides in me, and I in him. As the living Father sent me, and I live because of the Father, so *whoever feeds on me, he also will live because of me.* This is the bread that came down from heaven, not like the bread the fathers ate, and died. *Whoever feeds on this bread will live forever.'"

THE CROSS OF JESUS REPRESENTS A TABLE, AN ALTAR IF YOU will, that Jesus himself invites us to eat from all the days of our life. We know now, that this once difficult sermon, is talking about Jesus giving his flesh and blood at the cross for the sins of the world to reconcile us back to the Father. In this sermon he is teaching us a secret. There is a meal found at the cross. There is nourishment for our spirit if we can only learn to come and eat.

But how do we eat his flesh and how do we drink his blood?

We have to ask ourselves, what was God saying to us through the cross? What did God want us to know by giving his Son Jesus up to death for our sins?

"I love you. With everything that I have, I love you. I know you are in rebellion and sin against Me, but I want you to know that I love you so much that I was willing to sacrifice My own Son so that you could be forgiven, be born again into My family and enjoy fellowship with Me forever."

So Jesus is saying that the love of God, expressed through Jesus' own cross, is the spiritual meal that would nourish us and cause us to abide in him. So to eat his flesh and to drink his blood is to receive the love of God. It is to remember the love of God demonstrated on the cross, and to allow his love to penetrate your heart and saturate your very being.

Unfortunately, many of us object and resist God's love because we have judged ourselves according to the flesh. We have a list of sins, shortcomings and faults that in our own minds disqualify us from his love. We think, "I should know better by now." Or, "Surely God is disappointed with me that I have not been able to overcome this struggle." These thoughts are not from God and they keep you from receiving the love of God. We must repent and change our minds. God loves you and me and he demonstrated that love by sending Jesus to die on a cross to take away sin, sickness and death.

It is in remembering Jesus' agony, his brutal death on the cross, that our numb hearts are jolted back to life and awakened to his divine love. This 30-day journey is designed to help you remember his cross, to eat his flesh, to drink his blood and to receive the love of God.

THE TABLE OF THE LORD

"For I received from the Lord what I also delivered to you, that the Lord Jesus on the night when he was betrayed took bread, and when he had given thanks, he broke it, and said, 'This is my body, which is for you. Do this in remembrance of me.' In the same way also he took the cup, after supper, saying, 'This cup is the new covenant in my blood. Do this, as often as you drink it, in remembrance of me.' For as often as you eat this bread and drink the cup, you proclaim the Lord's death until he comes." (1 Corinthians 11:23-26)

FINALLY, BEFORE YOU BEGIN THIS 30-DAY JOURNEY, I WANT to encourage you to take communion each time you come before the Lord. The physical act of taking Holy Communion will assist you in bringing the Lord's work to remembrance. Through taking communion, you are physically receiving the Lord's body and his blood. It is an act of faith that will help you receive his love and enjoy his abiding presence. Read this Scripture out loud, slowly, and then take the elements as you remember him and give thanks for his work. Not only will you recognize a profound increase of the Lord's grace upon your life through this, but you will also see the enemy subdued all around you. Because through the Holy Communion, we are also proclaiming the Lord's death until he comes. We are proclaiming his victory over sin and the devil, by his death, in every area of our lives. Victory in our relationships! Victory in our finances! Victory in our future!

DAY ONE

~

MORNING VERSE:

"But now in Christ Jesus you who once were far off have been brought near by the blood of Christ." (Ephesians 2:13)

EVENING VERSE:

"In him we have redemption through his blood, the forgiveness of our trespasses, according to the riches of his grace." (Ephesians 1:7)

MEDITATION

YOU WERE ONCE FAR OFF. FOR THE WEIGHT OF THIS VERSE to hit your heart, you must remember the feeling of being far from God. Of being cut off from the promises, from the new covenant. Your sin and brokenness blinded you and caused you to pull away from a loving God. But now in Christ Jesus, you have been brought near by the blood of Christ. It is his blood that constitutes your nearness. Not your good behavior. Not your feelings. His blood. This is your confidence for experiencing and enjoying the nearness of God throughout your day. Keep your eyes on the cross and your heart warmed to his blood and you will abide in him.

DAY TWO

~

MORNING VERSE:

"I am the living bread that came down from heaven. If anyone eats of this bread, he will live forever. And the bread that I will give for the life of the world is my flesh." (John 6:51)

EVENING VERSE:

"But God shows his love for us in that while we were still sinners, Christ died for us." (Romans 5:8)

MEDITATION

WHEN YOU EAT A MEAL, YOUR BODY IS NOURISHED. YOU CAN feel the food convert to energy within your body. It quickens your mortal body and gives you strength to perform your daily duties. Anyone who has fasted understands the lethargy and fatigue that the body feels. So too, with your spirit. If you fast from the bread of God, your spirit will become lethargic and sleepy. To strengthen our spirits we must learn to eat the bread of God. To receive his broken body as the highest expression of love towards us. Take time to meditate on the agony and pain that Jesus endured to give us his flesh. If he endured so much to give us his flesh, how deep must his love for you be?

DAY THREE

~

MORNING VERSE:

"Therefore, as one trespass led to condemnation for all men, so one act of righteousness leads to justification and life for all men." (Romans 5:18)

EVENING VERSE:

"Do you not know that all of us who have been baptized into Christ Jesus were baptized into his death?" (Romans 6:3)

MEDITATION

BAPTISM INTO DEATH. YOUR BAPTISM WAS MORE THAN A public ceremony. It was a union. Your sinfulness, brokenness and depravity buried forever in the grave of Jesus. You rejoice in the cross because your sins were forgiven. But you must also learn to rejoice in the grave, for there your *sinfulness* was buried. Once and for all, Jesus took your old "operating system" of sinfulness and buried it in the grave. When he rose from the grave he gave you a new operating system called *righteousness*. The laws of God written on your heart and mind. Instead of trying so hard to overcome your sinfulness, trust that it has been buried once and for all through Jesus' death.

DAY FOUR

~

MORNING VERSE:

"For you have died, and your life is hidden with Christ in God." (Colossians 3:3)

EVENING VERSE:

"...and through him to reconcile to himself all things, whether on earth or in heaven, making peace by the blood of his cross." (Colossians 1:20)

MEDITATION

YOU HAVE DIED. LET IT SINK IN. EVERY FIBER OF YOUR OLD man has died. The part of you that resists God...dead. The part of you that lusts after the flesh...dead. The part of you that is selfish...dead. You have died. This truth is to be received by faith and the experience of it will come thereafter. The righteous shall live by faith. Think about the areas of your life that you are frustrated with, that you know do not please God. Think about the generational sins and habits that you received from your forefathers. Now picture all of it, joined to the lifeless body of Jesus Christ in the grave. You have died. Your life is now in Christ. To live is Christ, to die is gain.

DAY FIVE

~

MORNING VERSE:

"And you, who once were alienated and hostile in mind, doing evil deeds, he has now reconciled in his body of flesh by his death, in order to present you holy and blameless and above reproach before him." (Colossians 1:21-22)

EVENING VERSE:

"In him also you were circumcised with a circumcision made without hands, by putting off the body of the flesh, by the circumcision of Christ, having been buried with him in baptism..." (Colossians 2:11-12)

MEDITATION

THE BOOK OF PROVERBS SAYS, TO THE HUNGRY EVEN WHAT IS bitter tastes sweet. Something happens when you take time to remember your alienation from God, your hostile thoughts and your evil deeds. The bitterness of those days remind you of the pain and darkness you used to live in. Take some time to sit in that darkness. As you do, bring the work of the cross into your mind. See his body of flesh, bruised and beaten for you. All of your sins and hostility being absorbed by the Son of God. It was in his body of flesh, his death, that took you out of darkness and into the light. God's great vision for your life is that you would stand holy and blameless before him. How great is the cleansing power of the blood!

DAY SIX

∼

MORNING VERSE:

"For God has not destined us for wrath, but to obtain salvation through our Lord Jesus Christ, who died for us so that whether we are awake or asleep we might live with him." (1 Thessalonians 5:9-10)

EVENING VERSE:

"...always carrying in the body the death of Jesus, so that the life of Jesus may also be manifested in our bodies." (2 Corinthians 4:10)

MEDITATION

IN THE KINGDOM, LIFE COMES THROUGH DEATH. DO NOT BE dismayed or discouraged by the painful trials in your life. Don't waste a good trial! To fellowship with Christ in his suffering is a great privilege and is intended to bring life to you. To convert a trial into a blessing is a matter of perspective. You can complain and bemoan the trial, or you can enter into it and entrust yourself to the Father. Trials will cause you to either question the love of God or fall into it. It is easy to get confused in suffering when you lose sight of the cross. You start questioning the love of God, does he really care about you? Beloved, don't be deceived. He loves you so much! Don't lose faith and don't lose heart. Remember the Son.

DAY SEVEN

~

MORNING VERSE:

"For we who live are always being given over to death for Jesus' sake, so that the life of Jesus also may be manifested in our mortal flesh." (2 Corinthians 4:11)

EVENING VERSE:

"For the love of Christ controls us, because we have concluded this: that one has died for all, therefore all have died..." (2 Corinthians 5:14)

MEDITATION

WHAT WOULD YOUR LIFE LOOK LIKE CONTROLLED BY THE love of Christ? You may remember being controlled by anger or lust or some other thing. But the invitation today is for you to be controlled by the love of Christ! But how? You must make a conclusion. You must close the case. There is no room for being double minded on this matter. What conclusion must you make? *That One has died for all, therefore all have died.* You no longer relate to people based on their flesh, their sin or their selfishness. Because Jesus has died for you (and them) you have once and for all changed your mind about humanity. You will live in love because Christ died in love. It was the joy set before him that enabled him to endure the cross. You were and still are his joy!

DAY EIGHT

~

"Grace to you and peace from God our Father and the Lord Jesus Christ, who gave himself for our sins to deliver us from the present evil age..." (Galatians 1:3-4)

" I have been crucified with Christ. It is no longer I who live, but Christ who lives in me. And the life I now live in the flesh I live by faith in the Son of God, who loved me and gave himself for me." (Galatians 2:20)

MEDITATION

HAVE YOU REALLY BEEN CRUCIFIED? HAVE YOU SETTLED this issue in your heart? Are you still trying to overcome things that were crucified 2000 years ago? How much of your sin escaped the cross? What measure of brokenness were you able to sneak through the Lord's cross and his grave? If none, then beloved, why do you live as if it were so? You have been crucified with Christ. The life you live now, in the flesh, is to be lived by faith in the Son of God! He loves you and gave himself for you. Let hope arise! Let your affections be awakened to the depth and magnitude of his love. Quiet your heart. Take your eyes off of all the things that tempt you to despair, guilt and shame and turn your eyes to Jesus.

DAY NINE

~

MORNING VERSE:

"Christ redeemed us from the curse of the law by becoming a curse for us—for it is written, 'Cursed is everyone who is hanged on a tree.'" (Galatians 3:13)

EVENING VERSE:

"And those who belong to Christ Jesus have crucified the flesh with its passions and desires." (Galatians 5:24)

MEDITATION

YOU MAY FEEL AS THOUGH YOU DO NOT BELONG TO CHRIST, but it is only because you have wandered from his table. This promise is for those who belong. *Be. Long.* Belonging is a matter of being in the same place for a long time. This is the journey you are on, learning to be-long to Christ Jesus. What does it mean to belong to Christ Jesus? It means to be with him where he gave himself to us. It means to be joined to him, by faith, in every aspect of his work in saving us. Belonging speaks of being home and at rest. It is through your belonging to Christ, that the flesh is crucified and the passions and desires that once ruled your life are brought to nothing. Find your home at the cross, at the grave and in his resurrection. This is home. This is the table you are to eat from in order to grow up into salvation.

DAY TEN

~

MORNING VERSE:

"But far be it from me to boast except in the cross of our Lord Jesus Christ, by which the world has been crucified to me, and I to the world." (Galatians 6:14)

EVENING VERSE:

"For he himself is our peace, who has made us both one and has broken down in his flesh the dividing wall of hostility..." (Ephesians 2:14)

MEDITATION

WHAT DO YOU BOAST ABOUT? YOUR BOASTING IS NOT outward only. Your boasting is in every place that you function in your own strength. To the Apostle Paul, the thought of boasting in his own strength was anathema. To boast in the cross is to be constantly aware that all of your strength, blessings and goodness have come to you through the unconditional love of God expressed on the cross. David said, "I have no good apart from you." Your ability to make money, to do business, to love and to speak comes to you not on the basis of your natural strength. Has the world been crucified to you and have you been crucified to the world? Does the pride of life and desire for possessions dominate your affections? It is only by spending time, at the cross, in our hearts and minds that these lusts of the flesh are dealt with. There is no victory in trying harder! There is no victory and stacking up a list of spiritual things to do. The victory is in Jesus! It is in the cross. Slow down today and let the world be crucified to you, and you to the world.

DAY ELEVEN

~

MORNING VERSE:

"...and might reconcile us both to God in one body through the cross, thereby killing the hostility." (Ephesians 2:16)

EVENING VERSE:

"And walk in love, as Christ loved us and gave himself up for us, a fragrant offering and sacrifice to God." (Ephesians 5:2)

MEDITATION

OH THE BEAUTY AND LIFE THAT IS HIDDEN IN THE WORD OF God! Such brief phrases carry such weight and glory. Like a decanter to a nice bottle of wine, so is remembrance, meditation and thanksgiving to the Word of God. Slowing down to remember, to savor and enjoy God's work in saving you, will empower the Holy Spirit to bring out the nuance and color hidden beyond the black and white of the page. "*As Christ loved us.*" How did he love you? What manner of love is this? Who has ever loved you so perfectly as the Lord? The entire exhortation rests upon this phrase, "As Christ." The sum of Christian duty can be summed up in these two words..."as Christ." Let everything you do, be *as* Christ. Let it be a mirror of his life. Of his love. Of his humility and grace.

DAY TWELVE

~

MORNING VERSE:

"And all the people answered, 'His blood be on us and on our children!" Then he released for them Barabbas, and having scourged Jesus, delivered him to be crucified.'" (Matthew 27:25-26)

EVENING VERSE:

"And they stripped him and put a scarlet robe on him, and twisting together a crown of thorns, they put it on his head and put a reed in his right hand. And kneeling before him, they mocked him, saying, 'Hail, King of the Jews!'" (Matthew 27:28-29)

MEDITATION

I WAS NUMB TO THE CROSS AND THE LOVE OF GOD SO I ASKED him to awaken me to his love. To move this knowledge into an experiential reality. From the head to the heart. I heard the Father say, "Knowing what I did for you will have little power to change your life unless it is coupled with a deep understanding of why I did it." He was inviting me to revisit what I had always known and to ask him this simple question..."Why? Why did you do it? Why did you endure the mocking? The shame? The scourging?" This question has led me on a journey into the heart of God. Into the passion of Christ. As you walk through his crucifixion, find him every step of the way and ask him, "Why?".

DAY THIRTEEN

~

MORNING VERSE:

"And they spit on him and took the reed and struck him on the head. And when they had mocked him, they stripped him of the robe and put his own clothes on him and led him away to crucify him." (Matthew 27:30-31)

EVENING VERSE:

"And Jesus said, 'Father, forgive them, for they know not what they do.'" (Luke 23:34)

MEDITATION

HAVE YOU EXPERIENCED AN INJUSTICE? HAS SOMEONE YOU love deeply ever let you down? Ever repaid you evil for kindness? How did you respond? Perhaps even now you remember that you have put up some walls of offense towards loved ones who have betrayed you and let you down. Who have sinned grievously towards you. Your flesh is hurt. Your flesh demands justice and an apology. You have resolved that prior to offering forgiveness they must first repent and then change their behavior for some amount of time before you will forgive. Beloved, this attitude is earthly and is creating a prison around your own heart. Your pain is real, but do not exalt it above the Lord. Do not exalt your betrayal over the injustice of the cross. Hear the Lord's prayer again. "Father, forgive them, for they know not what they do." Forgive, as the Lord has forgiven you.

DAY FOURTEEN

~

MORNING VERSE:

"So Jesus came out, wearing the crown of thorns and the purple robe. Pilate said to them, 'Behold the man!' When the chief priests and the officers saw him, they cried out, 'Crucify him, crucify him!'" (John 19:5-6)

EVENING VERSE:

"When Jesus had received the sour wine, he said, 'It is finished,' and he bowed his head and gave up his spirit." (John 19:30)

MEDITATION

BEHOLD THE MAN! JESUS WAS ON A MISSION FROM THE Father to reconcile the world back into the family of God. Through his death, our sins were no longer counted against us. It wasn't that our sins weren't accounted for, it was that they were not counted *against* us. All of our sins were placed upon Jesus. Every single one of them accounted for...past, present and future. And when he said, "It is finished" He was telling you that the counting of sin is finished. There is no more counting. The reconciliation has been finalized. It is as if a down payment of a trillion dollars has been made and the only place you have to spend money is the dollar store. Your sin, even future ones, can never outweigh the blood of Jesus. So stop counting your sins, stop counting the sins of your loved ones, the church and the world and start praising Jesus! Start thanking God!

DAY FIFTEEN

~

MORNING VERSE:

"But one of the soldiers pierced his side with a spear, and at once there came out blood and water." (John 19:34)

EVENING VERSE:

"...this Jesus, delivered up according to the definite plan and foreknowledge of God, you crucified and killed by the hands of lawless men. God raised him up, loosing the pangs of death, because it was not possible for him to be held by it." (Acts 2:23-24)

MEDITATION

WHEN GOD AND ADAM SEARCHED CREATION TO FIND A helper suitable for him, none was found. God then caused a deep sleep to fall upon Adam, he opened his side and took out a rib from which he formed woman. This woman was born from Adam's side. Bone of his bone and flesh of his flesh. So too, when Jesus had fallen "asleep" on the cross, his side was opened and at once there came out blood and water. How is it that you are born again? Why, of course! You are born again through the blood of Jesus consummated through the waters of baptism! What a glorious picture! Just as Eve was born from Adam's side, so too the Bride of Christ is born from the Second Adam's side. This speaks of our union with Christ. Our new origin and our new end. Take time to meditate on this reality and recognize the confidence the Spirit intends to birth in you through this picture. The confidence that you have been born of God!

DAY SIXTEEN

~

MORNING VERSE:

"We were buried therefore with him by baptism into death, in order that, just as Christ was raised from the dead by the glory of the Father, we too might walk in newness of life." (Romans 6:4)

EVENING VERSE:

"For if we have been united with him in a death like his, we shall certainly be united with him in a resurrection like his." (Romans 6:5)

MEDITATION

THE SOLUTION FOR SINFULNESS IS THE GRAVE. THE WATERS of baptism represent and illustrate the fact that all of our sinfulness is buried once and for all. If the cross removes each of our sins, the grave removes our sinfulness. Just as Israel crossed safely through the Red Sea on dry land and Pharaoh and his army were buried, so too our taskmaster of sin was buried through the Lord's death. When you attempt to find freedom apart from identifying with the cross, the grave and his resurrection, you are in essence operating in unbelief. Take time to remember your water baptism. When you entered into the waters, you were declaring by faith that all of your sinfulness would be buried that day. As you came up out of the waters, you were joined in spirit to the Lord and his resurrection. You now have the power of the Spirit to live a new life! No longer controlled by sin, selfishness and death, but by the Spirit of God!

DAY SEVENTEEN

~

MORNING VERSE:

" For there is one God, and there is one mediator between God and men, the man Christ Jesus, who gave himself as a ransom for all..." (1 Timothy 2:5-6)

EVENING VERSE:

"...and which now has been manifested through the appearing of our Savior Christ Jesus, who abolished death and brought life and immortality to light through the gospel..." (2 Timothy 1:10)

MEDITATION

THERE IS A GROAN DEEP INSIDE EACH BORN AGAIN BELIEVER that longs for immortality and life. We instinctively rebel against the thought of death, knowing we were never made for it. It is through the appearing of Jesus Christ, that this longing deep within our spirits is confirmed. He triumphed over death, through the cross, and disarmed the devil through his wonderful salvation. For the believer, death has been abolished. It is no longer a dominating fear holding us captive. For the one who has died, is free from sin. How can death intimidate those who have died with Christ and been joined to him by the Holy Spirit? You were made by God for life and immortality. However, when you are faced with the reality of death, you are tempted to despair, to fear and to lose heart. Remember that Jesus holds the keys to

Death and Hades, that he has overcome the Devil once and for all and life and immortality is now our inheritance in him.

DAY EIGHTEEN

~

MORNING VERSE:

"If we have died with him, we will also live with him." (2 Timothy 2:11)

EVENING VERSE:

"...who gave himself for us to redeem us from all lawlessness and to purify for himself a people for his own possession who are zealous for good works." (Titus 2:14)

MEDITATION

IN THE KINGDOM, DEATH ALWAYS LEADS TO LIFE. THE farmer harvests his crops. In doing so, he kills the plant but gathers in food to bring life to his family and to others.

If you have died with him, you will also live with him. It is a big "if." Do you live as though you are dead to sin, or do you keep trying to wrestle with that *old man*? Do you trust that his cross has dealt with your brokenness once or for all or do you feel the need to add to his work? Beloved, stop trying to add to Jesus' work and receive it as if it is so. The righteous shall live by faith. To live with Christ is to live with righteousness, peace and joy. To live with Christ is to live with love, power and dominion. To live with Christ is your inheritance. By faith, let his resurrection life become your own.

DAY NINETEEN

~

MORNING VERSE:

"But when the goodness and loving kindness of God our Savior appeared, he saved us, not because of works done by us in righteousness, but according to his own mercy, by the washing of regeneration and renewal of the Holy Spirit..." (Titus 3:4-5)

EVENING VERSE:

"Since therefore the children share in flesh and blood, he himself likewise partook of the same things, that through death he might destroy the one who has the power of death, that is, the devil, and deliver all those who through fear of death were subject to lifelong slavery." (Hebrews 2:14-15)

MEDITATION

A SLAVE CANNOT GO WHERE HE PLEASES. FEAR IS A PRISON. Fear is a taskmaster. And the Devil held you, at one time, as a slave through the fear of death. This fear masters all those who have not come to Jesus. However, through the Gospel, a glorious freedom is revealed! The God-man, in humility, partook of flesh and blood. The Eternal One humbled himself to dwell in bodily form, being bound to time, space and all the other limitations and vulnerabilities of mankind. He partook of flesh and blood so that he could taste death for you. It is through his unlawful death, that the Devil has been destroyed. Though the Devil once had the power of death, he possesses it no longer. Take time to worship Jesus for his victory over the Devil. Thank him for his triumph. Rejoice in your salvation!

DAY TWENTY

~

MORNING VERSE:

"...he entered once for all into the holy places, not by means of the blood of goats and calves but by means of his own blood, thus securing an eternal redemption." (Hebrews 9:12)

EVENING VERSE:

"For if the blood of goats and bulls, and the sprinkling of defiled persons with the ashes of a heifer, sanctify for the purification of the flesh, how much more will the blood of Christ, who through the eternal Spirit offered himself without blemish to God, purify our conscience from dead works to serve the living God." (Hebrews 9:13-14)

MEDITATION

AS A PRIEST IN THE NEW COVENANT, YOU WERE MADE FOR nearness. You were made to draw close to God and to enjoy him forever. It is in his presence that there is fullness of joy. Are you lacking joy? Then you are lacking the consciousness of nearness. For it is impossible to be in the presence of God and be in want of joy. But how do you actually draw near? You know the Old Covenant priests were only able to enter the holy places, once a year and not without blood. But Jesus has entered into the true holy place, with his own blood, securing for us a path to draw near to God at all times. It is the consciousness of his blood, so superior to the blood of bulls and goats, that at any time we recall its efficacy, we may enjoy the presence of God.

DAY TWENTY-ONE

~

MORNING VERSE:

"Indeed, under the law almost everything is purified with blood, and without the shedding of blood there is no forgiveness of sins." (Hebrews 9:22)

EVENING VERSE:

"But as it is, he has appeared once for all at the end of the ages to put away sin by the sacrifice of himself." (Hebrews 9:26)

MEDITATION

DO YOU THINK OF YOURSELF AS PURE? DO YOU LOOK AT yourself in the mirror and smile at the vessel of honor that you have become? Everything is purified with blood. Have you ever wondered how the Holy Spirit is able to dwell in your mortal body and yet you are not consumed? What purity his blood must have wrought in your life for this to be true! Beloved, if you have taken your eyes off of his blood, if you have been blinded to its power, turn again to the precious cleansing power of Jesus' blood. Bring your blemishes before him, your weakness and your shame. Let his blood wash over you fresh and new today. Adore him. Worship him. Draw near to him.

DAY TWENTY-TWO

~

MORNING VERSE:

"And by that will we have been sanctified through the offering of the body of Jesus Christ once for all." (Hebrews 10:10)

EVENING VERSE:

"For my flesh is true food, and my blood is true drink. Whoever feeds on my flesh and drinks my blood abides in me, and I in him." (John 6:55-56)

MEDITATION

THIS IS THE TABLE YOU ARE LEARNING TO COME TO. THIS IS the meal you are learning to feed on. To come to the table is to remember his work on Calvary. To eat from the table is to allow his love to penetrate you. To come to the table is to remind your heart that he went to great lengths to demonstrate his love for you. To feed on his flesh and drink his blood is to allow the love of God to be poured into your heart by the Holy Spirit. To drink it in. To take him in. To be nourished into his likeness. The revelation of his passion for you is unto to you receiving the Lord himself. It is through this receiving of the Lord that you will discover the secret to fruitfulness in the kingdom.

DAY TWENTY-THREE

~

MORNING VERSE:

"'I will remember their sins and their lawless deeds no more.' Where there is forgiveness of these, there is no longer any offering for sin." (Hebrews 10:17-18)

EVENING VERSE:

"Therefore, brothers, since we have confidence to enter the holy places by the blood of Jesus, by the new and living way that he opened for us through the curtain, that is, through his flesh..." (Hebrews 10:19-20)

MEDITATION

DO YOU REMEMBER YOUR SINS? DOES THE DEVIL REMIND you *why God shouldn't love you?* Do family members like to bring up your past failures and mistakes? Though this may be true, let these words sink into your heart. God does not remember your sins or your lawless deeds! Because Christ has accounted for each and every one of them with his cross, the Father is satisfied. He is both just and the justifier of the one who has faith in Jesus! To remember your sin is to forget the cross. Don't live another day in the shadow of your past. You are not obligated to pay for what you did in the past, Christ has done that. If some part of your past still haunts you, let God's forgetfulness become your own.

DAY TWENTY-FOUR

~

MORNING VERSE:

"...knowing that you were ransomed from the futile ways inherited from your forefathers, not with perishable things such as silver or gold, but with the precious blood of Christ, like that of a lamb without blemish or spot." (1 Peter 1:18-19)

EVENING VERSE:

"He himself bore our sins in his body on the tree, that we might die to sin and live to righteousness. By his wounds you have been healed." (1 Peter 2:24)

MEDITATION

Do you know how valuable you are? Though no one on earth may perceive it or acknowledge it, you are more precious than you know! God thought it wise to spend the blood of his Son to bring you back into his family. You have been ransomed. You are not an orphan. You are not abandoned. You are not forgotten. The sins committed against you by your mother and father do not define you. You are not your past. You are not destined to follow in the footsteps of your forefathers because you have received a new bloodline, a new family. Take your time and thank Jesus for giving you a new family tree. You no longer have an uphill battle trying to overcome the sins of your family, you are a child of God.

DAY TWENTY-FIVE

~

MORNING VERSE:

"For Christ also suffered once for sins, the righteous for the unrighteous, that he might bring us to God, being put to death in the flesh but made alive in the spirit..." (1 Peter 3:18)

EVENING VERSE:

"Since therefore Christ suffered in the flesh, arm yourselves with the same way of thinking, for whoever has suffered in the flesh has ceased from sin, so as to live for the rest of the time in the flesh no longer for human passions but for the will of God." (1 Peter 4:1-2)

MEDITATION

THE 2ND AMENDMENT IN THE UNITED STATES constitution gives Americans the right to bear arms. However, in the kingdom, it is through a consciousness of Christ's sufferings that we are to arm our thinking! Why do we have to arm our thinking? Because that is where the battle lies! The world, the flesh and the Devil are constantly trying to get your thoughts on something other than Christ. This is especially true when you are suffering in some way! But, being mindful of Christ's sufferings, gives spirit-filled ammunition to your thoughts. You can shoot down discouragement, despair, unbelief and hopelessness. How? You can recognize that Christ also suffered and that what is happening to you is not strange or out of the ordinary but an opportunity for you to fellowship with him in his suffering!

DAY TWENTY-SIX

~

MORNING VERSE:

"Beloved, do not be surprised at the fiery trial when it comes upon you to test you, as though something strange were happening to you. But rejoice insofar as you share Christ's sufferings, that you may also rejoice and be glad when his glory is revealed." (1 Peter 4:12-13)

EVENING VERSE:

"For whoever lacks these qualities is so nearsighted that he is blind, having forgotten that he was cleansed from his former sins." (2 Peter 1:9)

MEDITATION

WHEN JESUS BEGAN HIS MINISTRY, HE QUOTES ISAIAH 61 which speaks of his anointing to proclaim good news to the poor, liberty to the captives, recovery of sight for the blind and liberty for the oppressed. Many of you have forgotten, grown cold and numb, to the glory of having been cleansed from your former sins. This forgetfulness has produced a spiritual blindness within you. But be encouraged! Jesus is still opening the eyes of the blind. Take time today and acknowledge your blindness before him. Tell him that you have forgotten how wonderful it is to be cleansed of your sin. If you have not forgotten, ask him simply to open your eyes even more and to help you to stay innocent and alive to the cleansing power of his blood.

DAY TWENTY-SEVEN

~

MORNING VERSE:

"He himself is the sacrifice that atones for our sins—and not only our sins but the sins of all the world." (1 John 2:2 NLT)

EVENING VERSE:

"You know that he appeared in order to take away sins, and in him there is no sin." (1 John 3:5)

MEDITATION

THERE ARE PEOPLE ALL AROUND YOU TODAY THAT DO NOT know that Jesus Christ has atoned for their sins. You are made to be a messenger of good news! His atonement does not just cover you beloved, it covers the sins of all the world. But blindly do they wander, still stuck in their sin, because they have not been told. The only thing that counts is faith expressing itself through love. Your act of love today is to share this good news with those who will listen. Remind them passionately that their sins have been atoned for! Give them an opportunity to put their faith in Jesus Christ! Take some time today and ask the Holy Spirit to lead you to someone who needs to hear this good news.

DAY TWENTY-EIGHT

~

MORNING VERSE:

"This is real love—not that we loved God, but that he loved us and sent his Son as a sacrifice to take away our sins. Dear friends, since God loved us that much, we surely ought to love each other." (1 John 4:10-11 NLT)

EVENING VERSE:

"This is he who came by water and blood—Jesus Christ; not by the water only but by the water and the blood." (1 John 5:6)

MEDITATION

To REPRESENT THE GOD OF LOVE WITHOUT LOVE IS hypocrisy. The evidence that we are truly learning to eat from the table of the Lord is a heart that is compelled to love his neighbor. You must let the river flow! If you receive God's unconditional love yet do not express it in word and deed to those around you, you will become a stagnant marsh. Fresh water flowing in, yet never flowing out. May it never be so! To become love is the highest calling because it is to become like our Master. You have been eating from the table of the Lord so that you, too, may endure your hour of betrayal and injustice. Forgive, as the Lord has forgiven you. Love, as the Lord has loved you.

DAY TWENTY-NINE

~

MORNING VERSE:

"We know that our old self was crucified with him in order that the body of sin might be brought to nothing, so that we would no longer be enslaved to sin." (Romans 6:6)

EVENING VERSE:

"For one who has died has been set free from sin." (Romans 6:7)

MEDITATION

GOD PROVIDES MANY OPPORTUNITIES FOR US TO WALK OUT what we say we believe. As you embrace your crucifixion with the Lord, you will likely face injustice. You will likely be sinned against in a way that tests your faith in this manner. Though the pain is real, you must bring it before the Father just like Jesus, and entrust yourself to the cup he is having you drink. You will drink his cup of suffering and you will enter into the glory of his resurrection. The key here is to remember that those sinning against you, are doing so because they have forgotten, even for a moment, who they are. Love is patient. So the first step of love is to offer patience. Love is kind. The second step of love is to offer kindness, even in their sin, knowing that God's kindness will lead men to repentance. Ask God to allow you to see others just as he does. Thank him for showing you kindness and mercy in the midst of your sin and rebellion and ask him for grace to offer the same.

DAY THIRTY

~

MORNING VERSE:

"He was despised and rejected by men, a man of sorrows and acquainted with grief; and as one from whom men hide their faces he was despised, and we esteemed him not." (Isaiah 53:3)

EVENING VERSE:

"Surely he has borne our griefs and carried our sorrows; yet we esteemed him stricken, smitten by God, and afflicted. But he was pierced for our transgressions; he was crushed for our iniquities; upon him was the chastisement that brought us peace, and with his wounds we are healed." (Isaiah 53:4-5)

MEDITATION

YOUR CHRIST HAS ENTERED INTO EVERY WEAKNESS, vulnerability and pain. There is nothing that you are feeling that he has not felt deeply. Do you grieve? He knows it well. Are you afflicted? He was afflicted more. Are you crushed by the weight and guilt of your sin? So was He. Are you sick? His wounds heal you. Stop hiding your weakness. Stop pretending you are okay. Bring yourself to the Lord, without hiding, and allow the Lamb of God to minister his touch to you. He promises you peace, healing and wholeness in every area of your life.

NOW THAT YOU HAVE FINISHED

CONGRATULATIONS FOR COMPLETING THIS 30-DAY JOURNEY! I trust that you are more alive and aware of God's love and presence than you were before you started. The good news is that this guide was designed for you to use repeatedly! Now that you have gone through it once, do it again, trying to memorize the verses as you go. This practice of remembrance will eventually become a part of your life. You will find yourself, throughout your day, bringing to mind the love of God demonstrated through the cross. It will impact how you treat other people. How you respond to suffering and how you love the world around you.

GRACE CHART RESOURCE

SOURCE OF GRACE	RESULT OF GRACE
He was tortured and beaten. Isaiah 53:4-5 Ephesians 2:11-22	This was for our **griefs, sorrows, sins, transgressions and iniquity.**
He was whipped across his back. Isaiah 53:5 Matthew 8:14-17	This saves us from **disease, sickness.**
He wore a crown of thorns. Genesis 3:18 John 19:2	The thorns were a **sign of the curse,** here he takes **the curse on our minds including depression and anxiety.**
He was nailed to a cross. Deuteronomy 21:23 1 Peter 1:18-19	Cursed is the one who is hung on a tree so **he takes every curse off our lives.**
His side was pierced and opened. Genesis 2:21-22 John 19:34 1 John 5:7-8	Like Adam's bride was taken from his side, so **the bride of Christ is born from the "Second Adam's" side.**
He gave up his spirit and died and he was buried. Romans 6 Galatians 2:20 2 Corinthians 5:17	**This death frees us from bondage to the flesh.** It destroys our sinful nature once and for all.
He was resurrected on the third day. Romans 6 Romans 8 Ephesians 4:17-24	This allows us to walk in newness of life, as new creatures. **We can walk by the Spirit once again.**

ALSO BY PETER LOUIS

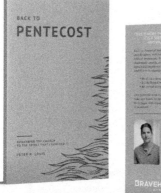

ABOUT THE AUTHOR

PETER K. LOUIS and his wife Kristi live in Dallas, Texas with their five children. He is the founder of *Braveheart Ministries*, a gospel-focused ministry focused on strengthening the faith of the Church and equipping the Body of Christ to walk in love. Peter enjoys spending time with his family, golfing, fishing and one day dreams of living on a farm.

FOR MORE INFORMATION ON **PETER LOUIS**
AND **BRAVEHEART MINISTRIES** VISIT:

BRAVEHEARTMINISTRIES.ORG

Made in the USA
Las Vegas, NV
19 December 2022

63511908R00059